PEOPLE WHO HELP US

Popcorn

Doctors

Honor Head

WAYLAND

D1514667

Explore the world with **Popcorn -** your complete first non-fiction library.

Look out for more titles in the Popcorn range. All books have the same format of simple text and striking images. Text is carefully matched to the pictures to help readers to identify and understand key vocabulary. www.waylandbooks.co.uk/popcorn

First published in 2010 by Wayland
Copyright © Wayland 2010

Wayland
Hachette Children's Books
338 Euston Road
London NW1 3BH

Wayland Australia
Level 17/207 Kent Street
Sydney NSW 2000

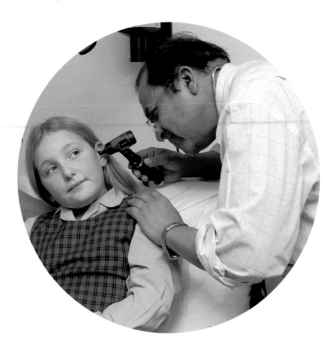

 Produced for Wayland by
White-Thomson Publishing Ltd
www.wtpub.co.uk
+44 (0)843 208 7460

Editor: Jean Coppendale
Designer: Clare Nicholas
Picture Researcher: Amy Sparks
Series consultant: Kate Ruttle
Consultant: Dr Robert Kirkpatrick
Design concept: Paul Cherrill

British Library Cataloguing in Publication Data
Head, Honor.
    Doctors. -- (Popcorn. People who help us)
    1. Physicians--Pictorial works--Juvenile literature.
    I. Title II. Series
    610.6'9-dc22

ISBN: 978 0 7502 6314 6

Wayland is a division of Hachette Children's Books,
an Hachette UK company.
www.hachette.co.uk

Printed and bound in China

Photographs:
Corbis: Adam Gault/Science Photo Library 9,
moodboard 16; Dreamstime: Yobro10 19/23tr; Franklin
Watts: Chris Fairclough 5, 7, 8; Getty Images: Peter
Dazeley 11/23tl, Jamie Kingham 20, Paul Burns 21;
iStockphoto: Sean Locke front cover; Photolibrary: LA/
VCHABEESIMPER 18; Shutterstock: 17, Hugo Silveirinha
Felix 6, Alexander Raths 1/10/23br, Monkey Business
Images 13, nehbitski 14/22; Wayland: Chris Fairclough
4, 2/12/23bl, 15

Contents

Your family doctor 4

Seeing the doctor 6

The doctor's room 8

What's wrong? 10

Ears and throat 12

Getting better 14

Practice nurse 16

Home visits 18

Hospital doctors 20

How do doctors help us? 22

Glossary 24

Index 24

Your family doctor

A family doctor is someone who
can help you when you are sick
or when you have hurt yourself.

The family doctor may look
after the whole family.

Your family doctor might work in a medical centre. Usually more than one doctor works here.

A medical centre might have a big reception where people have to check in.

Some family doctors work together in a practice.

Seeing the doctor

People usually have to make an
appointment to see the doctor.
They telephone the receptionist
at the doctor's practice
to arrange a time.

When someone feels
ill, they will phone
to make a doctor's
appointment.

**A person
going to see
the doctor
is called a
patient.**

Patients sit in the waiting room
until the doctor is ready to see them.
Some waiting rooms have toys, games
and books for children.

Most waiting rooms have magazines for patients
to read while they wait to see the doctor.

The doctor's room

When the doctor is ready, he calls the patient into his room. He may need to check the patient's medical notes.

The patient's medical notes tell the doctor why the patient has been to see him before.

The patient sits down to talk
to the doctor. The doctor will
ask the patient what the problem
is. Sometimes patients visit just
for a check up.

The doctor will
ask the patient
some questions.

What's wrong?

The doctor examines the patient to find out what is wrong. She may use some special equipment.

The doctor uses a stethoscope to check the patient's breathing.

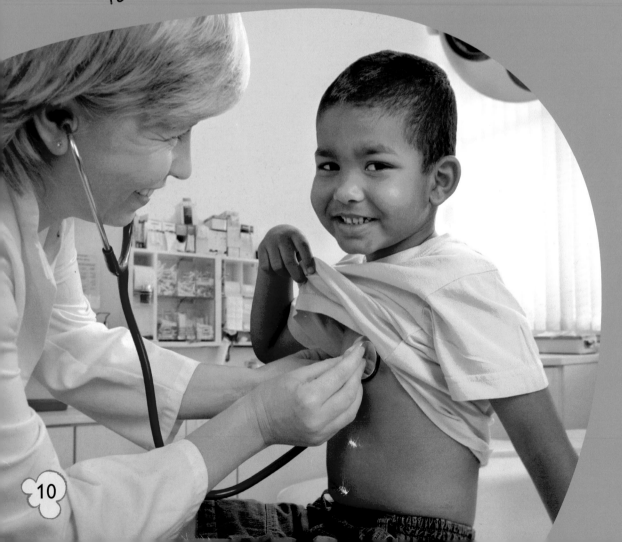

Sometimes the doctor will take the patient's temperature. She does this with a thermometer.

This thermometer goes just inside the patient's ear.

Before and after the examination the doctor will wash her hands so that she doesn't spread germs.

Ears and throat

This patient says she has an earache. The doctor looks inside her ear using an otoscope.

The otoscope shines a light into the patient's ear.

An otoscope helps the doctor to see if there is anything wrong inside a patient's ears.

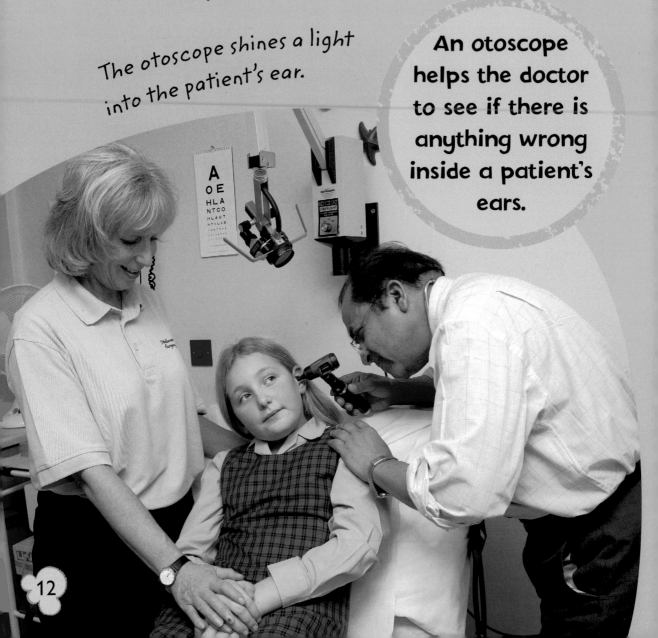

If the patient has a sore throat,
the doctor will look at the back
of the patient's throat.

The doctor uses a tongue depressor so
she can see the patient's throat clearly.

Getting better

When the doctor knows what is wrong he might write a prescription. This is a list of medicines to help make the patient better.

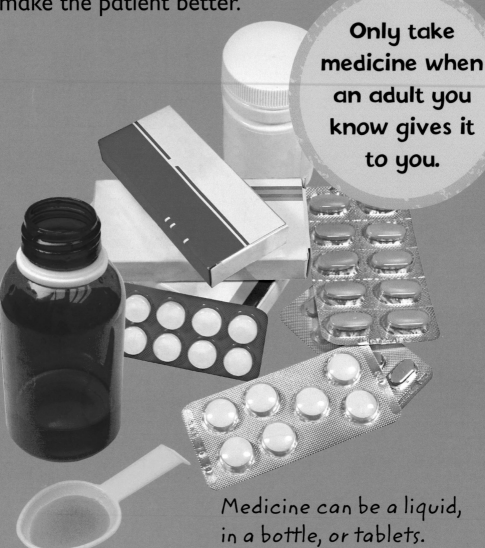

Only take medicine when an adult you know gives it to you.

Medicine can be a liquid, in a bottle, or tablets.

Sometimes the patient has to see a specialist. This is a doctor who knows more about a certain part of the body or disease.

This doctor is a skin specialist.

Practise nurse

Some doctors have nurses that help them. The nurse has her own room where she sees patients.

This nurse is giving a patient an immunisation.

Some nurses run a baby clinic at the practice. If there is a problem with the baby, the nurse will ask the doctor for help.

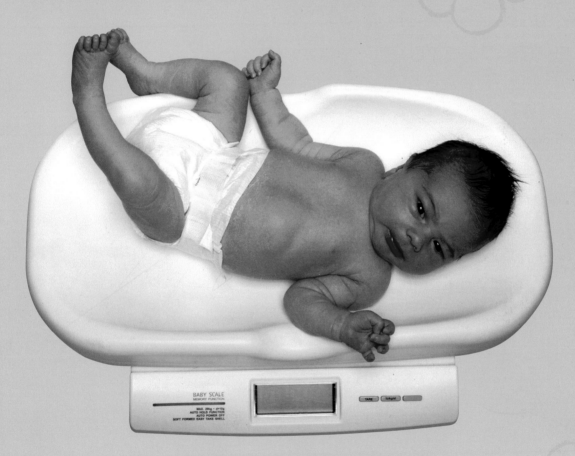

This baby is being weighed to make sure she is growing properly.

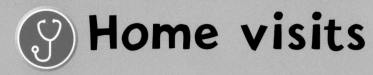 Home visits

Sometimes a patient is too sick to go to the doctor. Then the doctor will visit the patient at home.

A special bag has everything the doctor needs for a home visit.

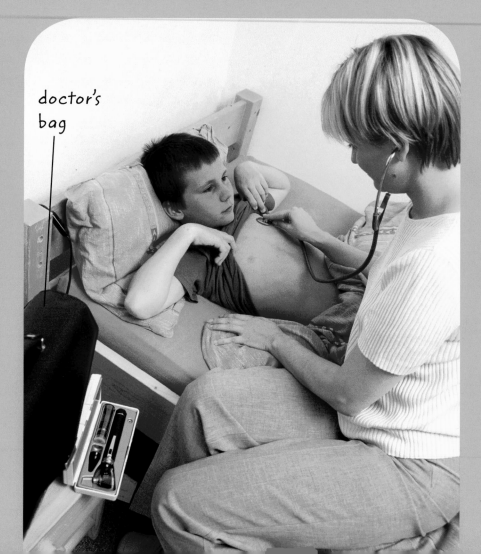

doctor's bag

If the person is very ill or needs special attention, the doctor may say the patient has to go to hospital.

The doctor calls for an ambulance to take the patient to hospital.

Hospital doctors

At the hospital the patient goes to the Accident and Emergency department or Outpatients. The patient will now be seen by a hospital doctor.

A hospital doctor will check the patient before deciding if the patient needs to stay in hospital.

At the hospital some doctor's specialise in looking after children. These doctors are called paediatricians.

Hospital doctors may check on their patients twice a day.

Most children in hospital stay in a special children's ward.

How do doctors help us?

Can you remember what doctors do to help us?
Match the pictures to the jobs below to find out.

1. Checks our breathing.

2. Writes a prescription for medicine
   to make us better.

3. Calls an ambulance if
   we are very sick.

4. Checks our ears if we
   have an earache.

5. Takes our
   temperature.

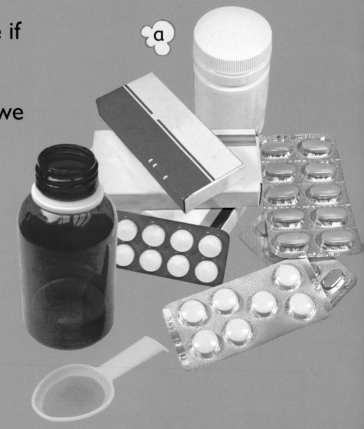

b

c

d

e

Glossary

appointment the date and time booked for a patient to see the doctor or nurse

check up an examination to help make sure the patient is well

clinic a place where you can go to see a doctor, specialist or nurse

disease something that makes you ill

examine to check the patient to find out what is wrong

immunisation something that stops a patient getting an illness

receptionist a person who helps the doctor by making appointments and looking after the medical notes

temperature how hot or cold your body is

ward a place in a hospital with lots of beds where patients stay

Index

ambulance 19

appointment 6

baby clinic 16

check up 9

earache 12

germs 11

hospital 19, 20-21

immunisation 16

medical centre 5

medical notes 8

medicine 14

otoscope 12

paediatrician 21

prescription 14

reception 5

sore throat 13

specialist 15

stethoscope 10

temperature 11

thermometer 11

tongue depressor 13

waiting room 7

People Who Help Us

Contents of titles in the series:

Ambulance Crew 978 07502 6313 9
Ambulance
The crew
Emergency!
Ambulance equipment
A road accident
In the ambulance
First responders
Calling an ambulance
St John Ambulance
How does an ambulance crew help us?
Glossary
Index

Doctors 978 07502 6314 6
Your local doctor
Seeing the doctor
The doctor's room
What's wrong?
Ears and throat
Getting better
Practice nurse
Home visits
Hospital doctors
How do doctors help us?
Glossary
Index

Firefighters 978 07502 6312 2
Firefighters
Fire engines
Fire!
Team work
Firefighting kit
Road accident
Trapped!
Calling 999
Staying safe
How do firefighters help us?
Glossary
Index

Police 978 07502 6311 5
Police officers
On the street
Emergency!
The police station
Crime scene
Police cars
Police motorbikes
Dog handlers
Mounted police
How do police help us?
Glossary
Index

WAYLAND